table of contents

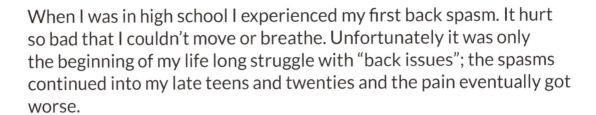

When I was in high school I experienced my first back spasm. It hurt so bad that I couldn't move or breathe. Unfortunately it was only the beginning of my life long struggle with "back issues"; the spasms continued into my late teens and twenties and the pain eventually got worse.

When I was pregnant with my daughter (my third child), my back pretty much went out in my first trimester. Sleep was torture and I was uncomfortable for about 7 of the 8ish months I was pregnant (she was born at 36 weeks) and I was in pain and out of alignment until after she was born. And by the time my fourth and last baby came along, I was a frequent visitor at my chiropractor's office for regular "adjustments".

My back issues were further exacerbated a few years ago when my car was rear-ended three times in a two year period.

I've had to live with the physical pain that comes from a misaligned body. When my hips and back are "off" or kiddywampus (as my MIL would say) and my body hurts, I go in for an adjustment to get realigned and I feel relief.

But I've realized, both in my own life and in the lives of clients I coach, the same thing happens when our lives get out of alignment.

Even worse than physical pain is the pain that comes from a **life that is out of alignment.**

Life hurts or at the very least can feel really uncomfortable or "off" when our time, habits, and actions do not align with our core values, passions and priorities. We just don't feel "right" until we are truly living what we believe with purpose and passion.

There is a soul ache that comes from a misaligned life. And a misaligned life can become a misaligned family.

I had my first child when I was 18, and by the time I was 21 I was a single mom of two boys. During my early years of motherhood, I rarely thought of the home culture that I wanted to create for my little family unit. Life then was about survival --I was going to college full-time, working full-time and being a mom. I thought I had to do it all and I thought I had to do all things at the same time.

This year my oldest child turned 18, and as I looked back I was saddened by what I consider to be the years of missed opportunity. Because we were in survival mode I was not intentional about what I wanted our family to be about. I only did what I thought I needed to do; I didn't know at the time how to make motherhood my own.

After I got remarried and we added two more children to our family (for a total of 4 kids), I decided there had to be another way. I was not a "victim" of motherhood, destined to go through the motions and raise my children according to what society deemed right. I was the designer of our home, and our values were its building blocks. .

Just like our bodies can ache when out of alignment, our families will suffer when our time, habits and actions are not aligned with our core values, passions and priorities. Yet I know from working with so many families that when life gets busy, implementing a plan where our values are consistently applied in our home culture can be tricky. This workbook is a product of my own journey to create a home culture where our actions, habits and family traditions are all aligned with our core values — *those things* we believe to be most important — but also as a result of the need for a guide to help families address the question "what do WE want to be *about*?"

In this book we'll be defining the qualities that make our families unique. We'll then go over some of the building blocks needed to establish a foundation on which to build our home culture and finally I'll share some intentional activities and exercises designed to get and keep your family in proper alignment.

This workbook will serve you to identify
- your family's uniqueness;
- your strengths and talents
- and your core values

The exercises in the book will help you create a vision for your family so that your children will leave home with a little "backpack" containing your values and meaningful traditions. By creating concrete goals that are aligned with your values, your family will make the most of the years you have together

In **part 1** we will walk through defining your family's values and creating a lexicon that is unique to your home culture. This will create the foundation that will be used to craft your aligned home.

In **part 2** we will take the word bank you've identified and build on those concepts by designing the framework your family will operate from. We will cover some key building blocks needed to establish a firm foundation for building a family and home culture that is in line with what you deem most important.

In **part 3** we will put all of the pieces together and look at some helpful tools for living with alignment of values and actions -- essentially creating meaningful practices to keep your family living out what you believe.

I hope you will refer back to this workbook often and that you will keep it tucked in a drawer and update it as your family grows. And that by the time your children leave home it will be dog-eared and coffee-stained from use.

PART 1

define

Determining the Target & Setting the Course

One of the exercises I frequently do with clients involves permission slips. I've found that often the biggest obstacle to change is our own expectation of what "should" be or where we "should" be at. So before moving forward with this workbook, let's look at what permission we may need to give ourselves and what expectations we may need to let go of to change our family's trajectory.

This can be a challenge as it might seem overly simplistic, but at the same time I think many of us live with our breath held, waiting for someone else to give us permission when it's truly ours to take.

Some examples:
- Permission to mess up
- Permission to fail and try again
- Permission to not do what other families are doing
- Permission to stop apologizing
- Permission to break stereotypes

What permissions do you need to give yourself in order to create a home environment that aligns with what's most important to YOUR family?

_____

_____

Now let's take moment for **Honest** reflection. Deep breath.

Something is not working.

And I don't know what your something is but here are a few of mine:
- My time and my priorities are not in line with each other
- I spend time on things that add no value, and feel stressed to accomplish other tasks
- I say yes to things that are not my best and often have to say no to things I'd love to do because I have over-committed

We need to be brutally honest about where we have gotten off course before being able to move forward and do something about it.

We can get so caught up in the flow of life that we can miss the opportunities to stop, breathe and say "Enough, I don't want to continue that way".

I can get set in the discomfort of my life, thinking "It's OK; I don't really need to do anything - things will just work out, right?"

But meanwhile, time passes by and nothing changes because I kid myself into thinking that change will magically happen from some outside source rather than taking ownership of the situation.

· Reflection Questions ·

Where in your family life are you sensing a need for a change?

_____

_____

_____

_____

_____

_____

_____

_____

Where you sensing that things have gotten out of alignment?

_____

_____

_____

_____

_____

_____

_____

_____

_____

Now that we have given ourselves permission to move forward I want to start with talking about strengths, and why it's important to parent from our strengths. In parenting, I think often it's much easier to focus on our weaknesses and play the comparison game.

For example, one of my very dear friends is an organization queen. She loves organizing and even vacuums out her junk drawers. I would love to be like that but *I'm not*. While I appreciate organization, I have a higher tolerance for mess and organizing is just not at the top of my strengths. We are uniquely made and our strengths play a part in our families.

Our strengths are a key ingredient, as are those of our spouse and children. Together we create the perfect **team**. When we focus on our weaknesses we get paralyzed, stuck. I wish I was more (fill in the blank) but I'm not so then what??? These thoughts only waste valuable time and energy whereas identifying and parenting from our strengths keeps us moving forward.

Grab a cup of coffee or tea and your journal and circle some of your tops strengths in the following worksheet. I invite you to print out an additional copy for your spouse as well.

identifying strengths

God created you with unique gifts, talents, and strengths. We were not all created to be good at every single thing. Your strengths are your personal characteristics that God can use to bless others. They are a part of who you are . . .

If you can identify your strengths and focus on applying them in your home, work, or personal interests you are much more likely to succeed.

Take 5 Minutes to circle three to five strengths that apply to you from the list below.

Adventurous	Energetic	Logical	Resourceful
Analytical	Enthusiastic	Loving	Responsible
Artistic	Fair	Loyal	Risk Taker
Athletic	Flexible	Manager	Sensitive
Brave	Focused	Mature	Self-assured
Calm	Forgiving	Math/Numbers	Servant-
Capable	Friendly	Multi-tasker	hearted
Caring	Frugal	Open	Serious
Cheerful	Funny	Optimistic	Spontaneous
Communication	Gentle	Organized	Supportive
Considerate	Gracious	Patient	Team Player
Courageous	Generous	Persuasive	Thoughtful
Creative	Hardworking	Planner	Trustworthy
Dedicated	Helpful	Positive	Visualization
Detail Oriented	Honest	Practical	Wise
Determined	Hospitable	Problem Solver	
Direct	Independent	Protective	*Add your own...*
Disciplined	Inspiring	Reflective	_____
Easygoing	Intelligent	Reliable	_____
Efficient	Kind	Resilient	_____
Encouraging	Listener	Respectful	_____

· Reflection Questions ·

identifying strengths

What were your top strengths?

_____

_____

_____

_____

_____

_____

_____

How do your strengths complement your spouse's?

_____

_____

_____

_____

_____

_____

_____

_____

When combined with our spouse's strengths these can set the tone as we set out to live and parent with purpose, authenticity and alignment. So take a minute to let your strengths sink in and be OK with them. It's not a competition; we are all different and have different wonderful strengths. We also want to be able to identify strengths in our children as they begin to emerge in their personalities.

As an additional resource consider taking the StrengthsFinders Assessment.This is a good tool for understanding your strengths and giving you a common language to express them. There is a small fee for taking it, but it is worth it.

Reflecting on Family of Origin

I don't know all the details of your story. But I know that like me, the details have shaped and impacted the person that you are today.

I'm sure no matter what your family history; there have been peaks and valleys. Some hard times and some amazing experiences.

We bring our past experiences into our current environments. And as we move forward with our desire to create a family culture that is unique to our strengths and values, we will glance back to look at where we came from and determine how we use those experiences to affect where we want our own families to go.

Use the following worksheet to think back on your childhood experiences. Consider what your family did that was great, that you loved and want to continue to do with your own family. Also think about what you did that you didn't enjoy, what you wish you had done more of and what you never did but wish you had.

looking back/looking ahead

What I LOVED from my family of origin and want to include with my own family	What I wish I would have done more of with my family of origin and want to do with my family now
What I never did with my family of origin that I would like to do with my family now	**What I did with my family of origin that I did not enjoy and do NOT want to do with my own family**

We bring our past experiences into our current environments.

Family Values

Our strengths and past experiences are a launching point. Now it's time to define what is most important in your family. What do we want our family to be about?

What values do we want our kids to leave home with in 18 years? This will help to create a map of how we want to navigate our family through life. For example, do you value fun? Perhaps you'll want to prioritize family fun dates or activities. Do you value hard work? You may incorporate family chores early on. Respect for the environment? You will probably make ecology and environmental education an important part of your family. Is faith a priority? If so, regular church attendance may be at the top of your list.

These values may change or evolve over time and that's OK. For example, we started out with education being at the top of our list. Right, education is a good thing and it was really important to us, but over time we realized that what we really valued was learning, so that took over that spot and slightly changed the course for our family.

In the following worksheet consider what your family values most.

family values worksheet

Abundance	Environment	Justice	Risk-taking
Acceptance	Equality	Kindness	Safety
Accomplishment	Ethics	Knowledge	Security
Accountability	Excellence	Leadership	Self-discipline
Achievement	Fairness	Learning	Self-expression
Adaptability	Faith	Legacy	Self-respect
Adventure	Family	Leisure	Serenity
Altruism	Financial	Love	Service
Ambition	stability	Loyalty	Simplicity
Authenticity	Flexibility	Making a	Spirituality
Balance	Forgiveness	difference	Sportsmanship
Beauty	Freedom	Obedience	Stewardship
Belonging	Friendship	Organization	Structure
Career	Fun	Openness	Success
Caring	Generosity	Optimism	Time
Cleanliness	Giving	Order	Teamwork
Collaboration	Grace	Nature	Thrift
Commitment	Gratitude	Parenting	Tradition
Community	Growth	Passion	Travel
Compassion	Harmony	Patriotism	Trust
Competence	Health	Patience	Truth
Confidence	Home	Peace	Understanding
Connection	Honesty	Perseverance	Uniqueness
Contentment	Hope	Personal	Usefulness
Contribution	Hospitality	fulfillment	Vision
Cooperation	Humility	Power	Wealth
Courage	Humor	Pride	Well-being
Creativity	Inclusion	Professionalism	Wholeheart-
Curiosity	Independence	Recognition	edness
Dignity	Influence	Reliability	Wisdom
Diversity	Integrity	Resilience	
Education	Initiative	Respect	*Add your own...*
Efficiency	Intuition	Resourcefulness	_____
Encouragement	Job security	Responsibility	_____
Empathy	Joy	Rest	

Behold, children are a heritage from the Lord,
  the fruit of the womb a reward.
Like arrows in the hand of a warrior
  are the children of one's youth.
Blessed is the man
  who fills his quiver with them!

Psalm 127:3-5

I love this verse because it's such a beautiful image of children as arrows. But it's made me think ... if children are our arrows, where are we aiming? What's the target?

At the end of their time in our home, what do we hope to have accomplished? What values, experiences and practical skills do we want them to leave with?

And, like arrows, our children will make an impact once they have been released. Where is our aim? What is the greatest goal and target for our children, for our family?

Our center target for our family is:

_____

_____

Other goals on the board include:

_____

_____

_____

If children are arrows in our quiver then we need to be prepared to pull back, release and let them fly. -zr

In addition to identifying your family's main target, consider also what specific tools, skills, experiences, and knowledge you want your child or children to one day leave home with. Imagine they will take with them a backpack filled with all of the experience they have.

aiming at the right target

What specific tools do I want my children to leave home with?

Practical Skills	Habits	Experiences	Values

PART 2

design

Crafting your home culture

Once you've determined what your target is for your family, it's time to dig in and start drafting the plans for creating your unique home culture and outlining the path that will take your arrows there.

Before you start planning, I want to address some common things that can get in the way and can cause your family to get off course.

Identifying the things that get in the way: Possible areas of adjustment

When there's a disconnect between what we value and how we live, it can often look something like this: our intentions are good, we have somewhat clear values and know what we want our lives to look like but… some things get in our way.

When we hurt ourselves, the injury can affect other parts of our bodies. One part of the body feeling "off" and we can quickly spiral downward. It may take medical care or a physical "adjustment" to get things back to their proper place. Likewise, when something feels "off" in our homes, it affects other pieces and it may take intentional adjustments to get things moving properly.

· Fear ·

Fear can be absolutely paralyzing. Fear of change, of making a wrong decision, of messing up our relationships, of not finding a job, of being alone. Often the actual outcome of addressing our fears is much less terrifying than the reality of doing nothing. It might feel safer to do nothing, but at what cost?

· Lack of Discipline ·

This is one I struggle with. I know what I'm supposed to do and if I actually set my mind to it and have some discipline I am able to eat healthy, exercise, and focus on key projects, but there are too many times when my mind wanders and I don't catch myself and get back on track. Intentional change requires discipline.

· Distractions ·

We sometimes feel overwhelmed because we have so many priorities that we don't feel like we can give any specific area all of our attention. How many times do we choose to "zone out", surf the internet, play a few rounds of Candy Crush, or just eat ice cream and have a movie marathon? Not that any of those things are bad on their own, but when we use them to numb because we're afraid of making a move or dealing with emotions, they can become roadblocks to living intentionally.

· Information Overload ·

Tell me if this sounds familiar at all to you. You sit down at the computer for "a few minutes" -- maybe you've got a project you want to work on, like you want to organize your garage. So you look for some ideas online, then head over to Pinterest for some more and before you know it you've spent several hours reading dozens of articles on organization. The number of hours actually spent organizing your garage? Zero. We live in a time of information overload. We can easily find facts, opinions, and personal narratives about every topic under the sun. And it can be paralyzing.

What barriers have affected our family's ability to stay in alignment?

_____

_____

_____

Just like our bones, muscles, and joints need to be in their proper place in order for our bodies to feel aligned; our families also depend on certain building blocks for a solid foundation that points in the right direction.

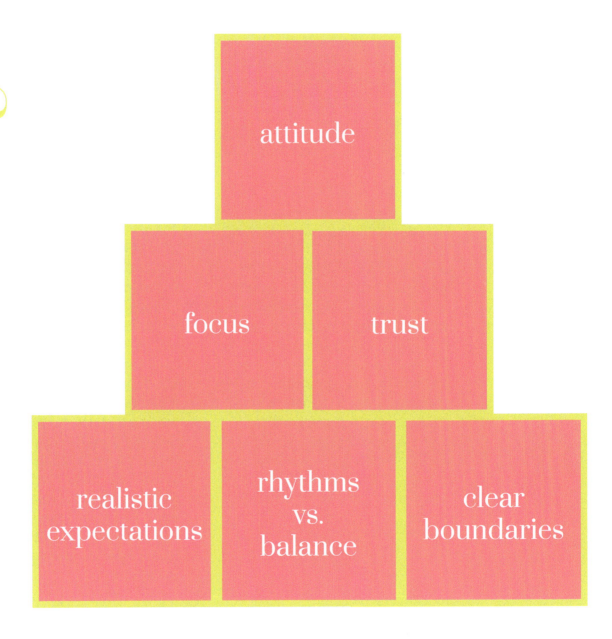

Several months ago when I was writing a series on my blog about a life "re-set" my husband commented on some changes he was noticing in me. He mentioned how happy he was that we were able to spend time together during the weekend and that I had been so willing to help him with things like weeding and staining our deck. He said all of this while I lay on the couch watching Monday night football with him, which he also commented, was out of character for me.

Why was I out gardening and staining and watching football? Because I love my husband, yes. But also because I had changed my attitude. I let go of the idea that I'm not outdoorsy or good at "gardening" and that I wouldn't be very good at staining our deck so why even offer to help.

I had to start seeing myself in a different way; as capable of many things even if they were things I had not spent time doing before. In order to get to a place where I could be intentional about a "reset" or truly living with alignment, I had to change my **attitude**.

Living with alignment involves having the right attitude.

In his book Mid-Course Correction Gordon MacDonald says this:

"Can anyone escape the patterns and attitudes that get us into trouble? Can anyone truly change?

Many are tempted to believe the answer is no, that there comes some critical moment in life when the development of a deeper, broader, more spirited life is no longer possible. And without thinking through the ramifications of their perception, they give up and abandon hope of all further transformation. Which, I say respectfully, is kind of stupid, certainly out of synch with what I hear Jesus, the Author of life-change, saying."

MacDonald uses the term *mid-course correction*. I'm using "realign" but they both refer to the "ways in which we seek to initiate change in our lives at any age and in any circumstance."

If we want to build a home that is in alignment with our values we need to believe that we are capable of change. Any past attitude of

Living with alignment involves having the right attitude.

defeat must be *replaced* with an attitude of hope and optimism. We must regain control of our quiver full of arrows and truly believe we are archers capable of shooting off our arrows in the right direction.

We are in a position to change our relationships, homes, circumstances, dreams. But we'll only get there if we actually believe we are capable of such things and do not allow outside influences to alter our attitudes.

· Consider ·

How has my attitude affected the direction our family has gone?

_____

_____

_____

_____

_____

_____

_____

_____

What beliefs about myself and/or our family do I need to adjust in order to move forward with creating an aligned home culture?

_____

_____

_____

_____

_____

_____

_____

_____

*What gets our attention determines our direction and, ultimately, our destination. Or if you would prefer the short version: **attention determines direction.***
Andy Stanley

We talked earlier about identifying our targets, right? Well imagine you are shooting an arrow at your target, how likely would it be that you would hit the target if you were not actually looking at it? Pretty unlikely. We'd need to focus on the target, keep our eyes on it and give it all of our attention.

Similarly where we end up in life 20, 30, or 40+ years from now depends on what has our attention right NOW.

Want to be a good parent? A good spouse, friend, worker? Then we need to keep our eyes on the road.

You know how when we're driving and we notice a car wreck off the side of the road and we can't help but look over and before we know it, we're starting to veer into the next lane? Yeah, life is like that, only with our time and our relationships.

We start off heading in the right direction with good intentions of living out our priorities but then. . .
- We want to get caught up on the latest episode(s) of our favorite show
- We sign our kids up for too many activities because everyone else is
- We say yes to volunteer for every single activity (because **they all** really need our help)
- We feel compelled to check our email 500 times a day (just in case of course)

Where we look determines the direction we go.

The thing is it feels good to be entertained. "Real life" can be so overwhelming at times that we need some kind of escape. But here's the thing, distractions are all about our "feelings" - what we feel, or what we're trying to avoid feeling. Giving our attention to the best things requires intentionality.

focus/attention

That child, spouse, friend, parent, or loved one who really needs your attention isn't going to wait forever. If they can't get it from you, they may start to look elsewhere, and you may lose your opportunity.

Living with intentionality does come with a cost, because when we "pay" attention to one thing we are not able to give that same attention to another. Let us not spend our lives "paying attention" to worthless pursuits. We can't get that time back.

The *decisions* we make today about what gets our attention will determine the direction our lives take.

This may be the right time to readjust our focus away from distractions and the "noise of life" and back onto our values, priorities and purpose - our MOST importants.

· Today Let's Consider ·

An honest look at what has our attention?

_____

_____

Are those things our best things?

_____

_____

Is there someone or something in our lives that is desperate for our attention that we have neglected?

_____

_____

Turn my eyes away from worthless things; preserve my life according to your word.

Psalm 119:3

trust/consistency

Trust is built in the very small moments.

Dr. Brené Brown

One of the most foundational pieces in building an aligned family is establishing a culture of trust in the home.

Trust is built over time by consistently doing what we say we will do. Imagine your child's piggy bank. Each time we are consistent with behavior that aligns with our values we make a deposit into the bank. But when we constantly break promises, we take huge handfuls of change out of our children's banks.

Yes, things do come up and there are times when we need to change plans and possibly break a promise. An environment of trust is one where those instances are the exception and not the rule.

Children need to know that they can trust our word. They also need to see our values put into action. If we say we value something but are not consistent about living it out, they will question whether it is something they need to value at all.

· Consider ·

How can I create an environment of trust in our home?

_____

_____

_____

Are there places where I need to work on re-building trust?

_____

_____

_____

Have you ever tried squeezing into jeans that were just a little too tight?

Ladies, I think you know what I'm talking about. You wiggle, tug and pull until you finally get them on and then you hold your breath and pray that you don't **come undone.**

Sometimes we do that with our lives. With our families. With our expectations.

We get it in our heads that our lives "should" be a certain way, our homes should look a certain way, and our kids should behave a certain way. Whether it be from cultural standards, media, comparing with our friends and neighbors, or looking to our families of origin — over time we develop EXPECTATIONS.

In a sense we stop looking for comfortable jeans and become determined to squeeze our lives into the smaller size that we think we "should" be able to fit into because I mean look at _____ (name of person you compare your life to), *they have it all together, they can fit into those jeans.*

Oh, expectations!

How often do we determine our success or value on the things we think we need to accomplish? And how often when we fail to accomplish such things do we end up feeling like failures?

I've had expectations that I've tried to squeeze into — I would have a certain kind of job by a certain point in my life; that my husband would be psychic and know exactly what I need at all times; that all four of my children would turn out easy and agreeable with minimal challenges, that my pregnancy weight would just magically come off right after I had babies, etc., etc.

You?

We often live with the idea that others around us (our families and loved ones) are aware of our expectations and can live up to them. When they fail to, it can cause all kinds of hurts in our relationships.

But worse than that, expectations can limit us from living out our full story. They can keep us in a box so that we measure our worth in comparison to others rather than fully exploring and accepting what God has planned for each of our lives.

That includes the good but also the painful, the disappointments and challenges that ultimately make us more resilient and more alive. We need to stop trying to land the part in someone else's story and start embracing our role as leading character in our own.

Don't get me wrong, not all expectations are bad. My children expect that I will feed them on a regular basis; my husband expects that I can be trusted to take care of our home; my mom expects that if she calls I'll answer or call her back. As a person of faith I expect that when I pray, God hears me.

But there may be some expectations that are a bit off for you right now. As we seek to design our unique home culture, there may be expectations that we need to let go of, adjust or better communicate.

- Maybe you're tired of squeezing yourself into someone else's life and it's time to realize yours is already pretty awesome.
- Maybe you need to ask for help with something instead of expecting that others "should just KNOW" what you need.
- Maybe it's time to own your story, the good and the challenging and expect all circumstances with an open heart.

*Consider where we might need to adjust our expectations. Are there any that you have been holding on to that are just unrealistic for this season or for **your** family.*

_____

_____

_____

_____

_____

_____

_____

rhythm vs. balance

Recently I was chatting with a friend who was feeling overwhelmed. She was tackling several projects and the conversation followed along the lines of what I often hear and have experienced myself, "I just feel like I have to DO. IT. ALL".

My friend was struggling to "balance" all of the projects, tasks and relationships in her life.

I asked her two simple questions, "do you have to do it ALL *right now*? And what would happen if you didn't?"

Because I've learned that I don't really believe in "balance". I think it's a good thing in theory but balance implies some kind of equal distribution of time, energy and resources.

And in reality, that's just not possible. We don't divide our 24 hours into equal slices of a pie where work, family, friends, activities, home projects and self-care all get a solid 4 hours. That would be *balance*.

Really, life more resembles a dance with rhythms, and consists of seasons.

One thing that is important as we embark on a realigned family is to think about in what *season* we find ourselves.

For example do we expect to be able to do everything in the same way we did after we:
- had children
- went back to school
- became a single parent
- went from one to two kids
- experienced a major health issue
- went back to work, etc

Life is made up of seasons. Some are busier than others, and there are some where more will be expected of us than others. There will be seasons when one relationship may need extra nurturing, or where one project may require extra time and attention, or when one dream may need to be put on hold for just a bit longer. There are times when work will require a greater slice of our time, others when a child may be sick or require extra attention, still others when we ourselves may need to make self-care a priority.

You can do anything, but not everything all at once.

I'm not sure who said that originally but it's so true, right?

One of the greatest changes in my life came about when I shifted my perspective from chasing "balance" in my life to embracing seasons.

· Take Some Time to Consider ·

What are some specific challenges or responsibilities you are facing in this season of your life?

_____

_____

_____

_____

*How can you show yourself more grace? Are there expectations that can be let go of **for a time**?*

_____

_____

_____

_____

Is there someone or something in our lives that is desperate for our attention that we have neglected?

_____

_____

_____

_____

The good is always the enemy of the best.
Oswald Chambers

If your family life is feeling a bit "off", there's a good chance that you also might have a hard time with boundaries.

Intentions are good, but they are not enough.

We live in a busy world with all kinds of ideas, opportunities, and information. It can be overwhelming, especially when thinking about how we spend our time.

When we give our time to something, whether it be offering to bake cookies for a school bake sale or saying yes when asked if you would join a church committee of some sort, we are taking away time from something else.

So we must consider: is this my best yes? Or is this just a good thing?

We must not confuse the command to love with the disease to please.
Lysa Terkeurst

I have a big extended family with lots of aunts, uncles and cousins so there is pretty much some birthday party or special family event happening almost every weekend.

When I was younger I let guilt influence my decisions and tried to attend as many events as I possibly could. This led to stress and ultimately some resentment to the point where I couldn't even enjoy going and spending time with family because I was thinking about the things I should be doing instead.

Once I became brave and learned about setting boundaries I started saying no. I love my extended family and enjoy spending time with them but I had to protect my own nuclear family's time. I still get guilt trips at times but have made it clear that it's not personal; we just have other commitments or just need some margin in our schedule and cannot attend all events.

clear boundaries

Saying "no" can be hard especially if we have not grown up doing it. It might feel uncomfortable but we need to remember that our yeses are valuable and they will end up taking away time from something else.

Whenever you say yes to something there is less of you for something else. Make sure your yes is worth the less.
Louie Giglio

Let's move forward by considering all the options competing for our time, and revisit our priorities and availability before signing up for something new or even continuing to participate in certain activities. Let's *resist* the pressure of saying yes to everything that gets presented to us. Let's free ourselves of the pressure to please others.

Choose discomfort over resentment.
Brene' Brown

There are so many good things, let's save our yeses for the BEST things. The things God has uniquely designed for each one of us.

· Consider ·

Do we have clear boundaries set in place to protect our family's time and integrity?

_____

_____

Are there things I may need to let go of that are not in line with our family's core values?

_____

_____

Are there ways I can practice saying no if that's been hard for me in the past?

_____

_____

PART 3

align

Tools for Aligned Living

In this final section I want to provide some practical tools to use as you seek to live out your aligned home culture and family dynamics. These exercises will be helpful for creating an action plan and implementing meaningful practices to keep your family living out what you value most.

A family mission statement is a combined, unified expression from all family members of what your family is about—what it is you really want to do and be—and the principles you choose to govern your family life.
Stephen Covey

STEP 1: SET A FAMILY MEETING
Whether it's just you and your spouse (if your children are young) or the whole family, set aside a time when you have a few hours to work on creating your family purpose statement.

STEP 2: ASK QUESTIONS AND DISCUSS WHAT YOUR FAMILY IS ALL ABOUT

What is the purpose of our family?

_____

_____

_____

What kind of family do we want to be?

_____

_____

_____

What kinds of things do we want to do?

_____

_____

_____

creating a family purpose statement

What do we want our home to feel like?

_____

_____

_____

What kind of home do we want to invite our friends to?

_____

_____

_____

What do we want to be remembered by?

_____

_____

_____

What kind of relationships do we want to have with one another?

_____

_____

_____

How do we want to treat one another and speak to one another?

_____

_____

_____

What are the unique talents, gifts, and abilities of family members?

_____

_____

_____

What are our responsibilities as family members?

_____

_____

_____

What are the principles and guidelines we want our family to follow?

_____

_____

_____

What are practical ways we can serve others outside our family?

_____

_____

_____

What are the top four priorities we want our family to value?

_____

_____

_____

STEP 3: REVIEW THE ANSWERS

Look at your responses and note any themes. Then look for a few descriptive words to describe your themes.

STEP 4: CREATE A DRAFT STATEMENT BASED ON YOUR ANSWERS

I recommend keeping it short, timeless, and applicable. If it's too vague, it won't really help in your day-to-day decision making but if it's too specific, it may become outdated or inapplicable over time.

(Example 1) We, the Jones family, believe that our purpose as a family is to live with Integrity. We will accomplish this by:
- valuing Honesty and Respect as our main guiding principles
- making our home a place of Rest, Laughter and Adventure
- prioritizing Love above lesser values
- interacting with each other in a spirit of Encouragement

Or

(Example 2) The Smith Family Mission Statement;
- To Love one another
- To Believe in one another
- To Use our time, talents and resources to bless others
- To Pray and Worship God together

Be creative and original! Let your statement reflect who you are as a family.

_____

_____

_____

_____

_____

_____

_____

_____

STEP 5

Display prominently in your home and refer back to it during family meetings, when setting family goals or as needed.

Now that we have identified a list of family values, we can be proactive about implementing them by creating family rules. It is important to identify rules to which we expect our children to be held accountable. Likewise, it can be beneficial to be proactive about setting appropriate consequences when rules are broken. This forms a system of accountability that relies less on impulse or emotion when rules are not followed, but sets up an opportunity to consistently live out and practice values.

Consider what rules would be most appropriate for your home based on ages of children and what consequences they can be held to.

You can start by identifying a list of behaviors that are important to your family, for example;
"We will tell the truth, show kindness, pick up after ourselves, etc."
Then use the list to answer the following prompt:

In this family we will:

_____

_____

_____

_____

Once you have created a basic set of rules take some time to consider appropriate consequences for breaking one of the rules;
Time-out, loss of a privilege, no desert, etc.

_____

_____

_____

_____

Identifying consequences before a rule is broken can help with diffusing a situation later on. If consequences are clearly stated the child will not be surprised because you've already discussed it before a conflict arose. It is also appropriate to take some time to think about a proper consequence if a new situation should arise.

skills training

Refer to the Backpack exercise in part 1. Look at the list of skills, experiences, and practical tools that you identified. In the chart below consider how you will move forward with training you child these skills.

Skill (Example; swimming)	Who will teach? Grandpa	When? Next Summer

We talked in section 2 about rhythms vs balance. Every season brings with it opportunities and limitations and when we can work within the framework of seasons we are better able to maximize our time.

I would guess that your calendar also moves with the seasons whether you are intentional about planning projects and goals around them or not.

If I break my calendar into 4 quarters, that gives me 4 unique opportunities to work on goals and projects.

In the following worksheets consider your own family's rhythms and seasons and the role they might play in how to be more intentional with your time.

Perhaps you have your own seasonal opportunities and limitations. Things like:
- work deadlines
- family celebrations, holidays, birthdays
- seasonal church or ministry responsibilities
- vacations
- back to school and end of school year events and responsibilities

If we can shift our focus away from the "must do it all right now" mentality to "I can do one or two specific tasks now and another one or two next month or next season" we will be able to make better progress, accomplish tangible results, live with more intention and be more present in our relationships.

Shift your focus away from the "must do it all now" mentality.

quarter 1

January · February · March

Opportunities *(example; vacation from school or work)*			
Limitations *(example; fall football practice 3x per week)*			
Activities *(example; serving at church for the holidays)*			
Goals *(example; work on front yard landscaping)*			
Traditions and Celebrations *(example; traveling to visit grandparents for their anniversary)*			

quarter 2

Opportunities *(example; vacation from school or work)*			
Limitations *(example; fall football practice 3x per week)*			
Activities *(example; serving at church for the holidays)*			
Goals *(example; work on front yard landscaping)*			
Traditions and Celebrations *(example; traveling to visit grandparents for their anniversary)*			

quarter 3

July · August · September

Opportunities *(example; vacation from school or work)*			
Limitations *(example; fall football practice 3x per week)*			
Activities *(example; serving at church for the holidays)*			
Goals *(example; work on front yard landscaping)*			
Traditions and Celebrations *(example; traveling to visit grandparents for their anniversary)*			

quarter 4

October · November · December

Opportunities *(example; vacation from school or work)*			
Limitations *(example; fall football practice 3x per week)*			
Activities *(example; serving at church for the holidays)*			
Goals *(example; work on front yard landscaping)*			
Traditions and Celebrations *(example; traveling to visit grandparents for their anniversary)*			

quarter planning overview

quarter 1

January	February	March

quarter 2

April	May	June

quarter 3

July	August	September

quarter 4

October	November	December

goals

OK friends, so as we adjust our expectations to be more aligned with our core values, we need to put that into practice. I don't know about you but we are a "list" kind of family so I have a daily to-do list that I adhere to for myself as well as adding in weekly time for working on larger projects.

To be honest one of my "secrets" is that I keep my to-do list intentionally short. I aim to accomplish 3 things, 5 max.

No matter how you tackle your to-do's I highly recommend going over your process with your values/priorities lenses on and taking some time to redesign your days so you are able to live more aligned.

Regarding goals, I like using SMART goals in my personal life and I encourage you to do the same.

SMART stands for:
- Specific
- Measureable
- Attainable
- Realistic & relevant
- Time-bound

Think about your personal and perhaps your family goals. I recommend short-term weekly, monthly, and quarterly goals as well as longer term 1 year, 5 year, 10 year goals.

For example: weekly family movie night, monthly service day, quarterly visit with grandparents, yearly family vacation.

How might you redesign your own goals and to-do lists in order to live more aligned with your values and priorities?

_____

_____

_____

_____

Use the following worksheets to help you plan your family goals.

s.m.a.r.t. goal worksheet

To get from where you are to where you would like to be, create SMART goals, they are:

Specific: Who? What? Does your goal clearly state what you are trying to achieve?

Measureable: How will you know if you are making progress? How will you know when you have reached your goal?

Achievable: Is achieving this goal realistic with effort and commitment? Have you got the resources to achieve this goal? If not, how will you get them?

Relevant: Does this goal reflect your values? Why is this goal significant to your life or for your family?

Time Bound: When will you reach your goal?

Below identify a few key goals that you would like to accomplish.

GOAL 1

_____

_____

GOAL 2

_____

_____

GOAL 3

_____

_____

GOAL 4

_____

_____

GOAL 5

_____

_____

Family traditions are a great way to celebrate the uniqueness of your family. Refer to the Looking Back/Looking Ahead worksheet in part 1. Think about family traditions and celebrations or rituals you would like to make a part of your home culture. On the chart below, think about the special occasions your family celebrates. On the right column, consider what rituals and traditions you would like to incorporate to make the occasion special.

Occasion	Tradition
Birthdays	
Anniversaries	
Back to School	
Vacation Breaks	
Holidays	
Religious celebrations	
Family Reunions	
Sports or activities	
Add your own	

family bucket list

What memories and experiences do we want to create together? In the list below brainstorm some of the activities and moments you would like to share as a family in the years you have at home together.

- _____
- _____
- _____
- _____
- _____
- _____
- _____
- _____
- _____
- _____
- _____
- _____
- _____
- _____
- _____
- _____
- _____
- _____
- _____

margin, rest & self-care

While we need to be proactive and intentional about the activities we engage in with our families; it is also just as important to allow for margin or "down-time" to just enjoy each other's company.

In the space below, identify the activities or lack of activity that would be most effective for restorative care for your family's needs.

Examples: weekly family movie night, monthly date night, and weekly personal time with friends. Or maybe even block off a time and NOT scheduling anything for Sunday afternoons as family/personal margin time.

Family Care	Marriage Care	Self-Care

conclusion

There is a lot of noise in the world and our kids will hear many different perspectives on what to value.

If we have clear values that guide our choices we will live with intention and meaning. Living with alignment means saying yes to the most important things and making time for them while limiting or eliminating some things that are just not within the sphere of our values.

We only have 18 years. 18 Summers. 18 Falls. 18 Winters and 18 Springs.

What will we do with them? Let's choose to be intentional and make sure our children know what WE value most. Because they will hear what we say but believe and imitate what we do.

At the beginning of the book I asked what permissions do you need to give yourself in order to create a home environment that aligns with what's most important to YOUR family? There's good chance that despite best intentions, you may find yourself starting to get out of alignment again at some point. Use the permission slips on the next page (as needed) to show yourself some grace, make necessary adjustments and get back on course. Examples; permission to say no to _____ (activity, commitment, project), permission to get take-out during a busy season or permission to take a hooky day with the kids and make memories.

And remember, *you've got this!*

parenting permission slips

I _____ *give myself/our family permission to:*

_____

_____

_____

_____

_____

I _____ *give myself/our family permission to:*

_____

_____

_____

_____

_____

I _____ *give myself/our family permission to:*

_____

_____

_____

_____

_____

resources

Boundaries: When to Say Yes, How to Say No to Take Control of Your Life
Dr. Henry Cloud & John Townsend

Boundaries with Kids: When to Say Yes, When to Say No, to Help Your Children Gain Control of Their Lives
Dr. Henry Cloud & John Townsend

Margin: Restoring Emotional, Physical, Financial, and Time Reserves to Overloaded Lives
Richard Swensen

Strengths Finder
Tom Rath

The 7 Habits of Highly Effective Families
Steven R. Covey

The Best Yes: Making Wise Decisions in the Midst of Endless Demands
Lysa Terkeurst

The Gifts of Imperfection
Dr. Brene' Brown

The Principle of the Path:
How to Get from Where You Are to Where You Want to Be
Andy Stanley

Your Life in Rhythm
Bruce B. Miller

notes

notes

Zohary Ross is a writer, speaker and life coach. She is passionate about living authentically and equipping and encouraging women to live "all in" with alignment of values, beliefs and actions and she tries to live out what she coaches. Her background is in counseling and education and she has a master's degree in counseling psychology and is a certified life coach as well as a certified Daring Way™ Facilitator—Candidate. She has a mild addiction to mint chocolate, office supplies (especially pens), and personality tests (she's a Nine on Enneagram and a ENFJ if you're into that sort of thing).

Zohary lives in the San Francisco Bay Area with her awesome husband and four children. Connect with her on her web site at zoharyross.com.

CPSIA information can be obtained
at www.ICGtesting.com
Printed in the USA
FSOW03n0140050216
16534FS